Copy 1

DISCARD

Churubusco Elementary School
Churubusco, Indiana 46723

what you will learn from this book

The TV screen shows the receiver gathering in a long pass just as he crosses the goal line. Maybe the pass was completed for the winning touchdown. Was this just an accident? Could anybody catch that ball?

This book will tell you how to catch a football. You will learn the skills needed to be a pass receiver. If you have some natural ability and work on what you learn in this book, you can become a good pass receiver.

1

catching the football

text/Paul J. Deegan
illustrations/
Harold Henriksen

Consultant: John Coatta, M.A., Physical Education, University of Wisconsin;
Assistant Professor of Physical Education, Mankato State College;
Head Football Coach, Mankato State College.

CREATIVE EDUCATION
Mankato, Minnesota

Published by Creative Educational Society, Inc., 123 South Broad Street,
Mankato, Minnesota 56001. Copyright © 1975 by Creative Educational Society,
Inc. International copyrights reserved in all countries. No part of this book may be
reproduced in any form without written permission from the publisher. Printed in
the United States. Distributed by Childrens Press, 1224 West Van Buren Street,
Chicago, Illinois 60607.
Library of Congress Number: 74-34572   ISBN: 0-87191-426-3
Library of Congress Cataloging in Publication Data
Deegan, Paul J 1937-   Catching the football.
    SUMMARY: Describes football catching techniques. 1. Passing (Football)—
Juvenile literature [1. Passing (Football) 2. Football]
I. Henriksen, Harold, ill.   II. Title. GV951.5.D43   796.33'225   74-34572
ISBN 0-87191-426-3

**For Lisa, Mike, and John – may participation in athletics bring
you as much enjoyment as it has brought your dad.**

FOOTBALL

There are three things you must keep in mind every time you catch a football. This is true in a sandlot game among young players and in the Super Bowl. Every time a receiver catches a ball, he or she must:

CATCH IT!
TUCK IT AWAY!
EXPLODE UP FIELD!

These are not always easy to do. Surprisingly perhaps, you will sometimes find it difficult to do them in the above order. And this is a must.

catch it!

tuck it away!

explode up field!

first make sure you catch it!

protect it!

It is natural for young receivers to think about running, perhaps even scoring a touchdown, when they think they're going to make the catch. There's nothing wrong with the idea but running is the third step. First the receiver must make sure of the catch. Then the ball must be protected for running. The result otherwise is likely to be a dropped ball or a fumble.

Catching the ball must be the receiver's number one goal. The play is over if the ball is not caught.

concentrate on the ball

Most dropped passes are due to lack of concentration. Watching football games, you have often seen a good pass bounce off a receiver's chest or shoulder pads. Sometimes a receiver simply drops a well-thrown ball. This is usually because the receiver's concentration was broken.

Good receivers have to learn to block everything from their mind except catching the ball. The next time you watch a pro game on TV take a close look at the pass receivers. See how intently they watch the ball as it comes to them.

When catching a pass, you must see the ball all the way into your hands. You must "look" the ball into your hands. If you give your full attention to this, your concentration will be hard to break.

It is harder to maintain concentration in some situations. That's why some pass patterns are called "courage routes." These are mostly patterns which take the receiver over the middle where coverage is by the linebackers. There's nothing a linebacker would rather do than get a good lick on a receiver. The successful receiver has to be able to concentrate only on catching the ball. He must not think about getting hammered while making the catch.

11

side

above

use your hands

in front

below

You want to catch a football with your hands. You do not want to trap the ball against your body. Young players often develop the bad habit of trapping the ball against their chest. Improper technique is difficult to unlearn.

If you have trouble controlling the ball in your hands, get hold of a junior-sized football. It is better to play with the slightly smaller ball and learn the correct technique.

It is easy to say: Catch the football with your hands. It's not always easy to remember how necessary this is. John Gilliam, one of the best wide receivers in pro football, realizes this. Talking about a long pass he felt he should have held on to during a game, Gilliam said: "But I caught it with my body and not with my hands."

13

The way to use your hands in catching a football is to make a basket out of them. Bring your hands close together. Hold the fingers up with the palms out. Let the thumbs touch. This is the basket you use to catch passes thrown right at you and above waist level.

If the ball is below waist level, turn the fingers down and bring your little fingers together.

Your fingers should be firm but not tense as you await the ball. You relax your hands the moment the ball arrives. Accept the ball into your hands. Welcome it.

Some boys and girls really have trouble catching the ball. Part of the reason is that their hands aren't relaxed. They're fighting the ball when it arrives. Athletes and coaches talk about "bad hands." Some players get nicknamed "iron hands." People's hands are not that different. It's what you learn to do with them that makes a difference.

Palms toward you

Little fingers together

Many passes of course will not be thrown directly at you. Often the pass will be to one side or the other. When possible, you should try to move your entire body so that you can catch the ball as we've talked about. If you can't but are still facing the ball, just reach out and form the pocket as we've described.

When you're not facing the passer and have your back to the ball, you'll always be taking the pass over a shoulder or over your head. In this situation, your palms are toward you, the fingers are up, and the little fingers are joined. If you're reaching to one side, the pocket will have one hand on the bottom and one on the top.

explode
up field

Reaching creates a problem for many receivers. If they're right-handed, they prefer to catch a ball over their left shoulder with the right hand on the bottom of the pocket. This is not the best way because it means reaching your arms across your body which is something you should not do.

The correct way to catch a ball over your left shoulder is with the right hand up, forming the top of the pocket. If a ball is coming over your right shoulder, the left hand is up.

To see why this is better, reach out to your right and form a pocket with your right hand on the bottom of the pocket. Now reach across your body to your left with your right hand still forming the bottom of the pocket. Notice that you could reach several inches farther when you reached to the right.

There's also another factor. When you bring your arms across your body, you block your vision. You may easily lose sight of the pass you're trying to catch.

On a low pass thrown at you, don't be afraid to dive or drop to your knees to make the catch. Be prepared to go after the ball. Many sideline turn-in passes are purposely thrown low to prevent interceptions.

During most football games, someone makes a spectacular catch. "Circus" catches they're often called. There's no way to learn these things. The gifted athlete does some of these things on instinct. Alertness and great desire also play a part.

Good receivers, though, are expected to catch the ball if they get their hands on it. They're also expected to make a tough catch once in a while. Most important, good receivers seldom drop the easy catch.

23

No catch will help your team if it's followed by a fumble. After catching a pass, you must put the ball in a protected position before running. The receiver carries the ball as a running back does in the open field.

The ball is carried in one hand. The fingers are over the forward tip of the ball. The middle finger (the largest one) and the index finger (the one next to the thumb) are split, one going on each side of the tip. The fingers grip the ball firmly. This forms one pocket for the ball.

The other end of the ball is pushed back against a pocket formed by the crotch of the elbow and the upper arm. The ball is jammed against this pocket. Held this way, the football cannot easily be jarred loose.

Now you are ready to run with the ball. After a catch, you may only need to run forward. Sometimes you'll need to make a move to free yourself from defensive players. This is usually necessary when you've made the catch facing the passer. A fake with the head and shoulders in one direction and a quick pivot in the other direction will often give you running room.

The roles of different receivers and pass patterns will be discussed fully in another book on the overall passing game. Each receiver, though, must get free to catch a pass. To do this, you must learn to do a couple of things well.

The most important thing if you line up on or close to the line of scrimmage is to blast off the line. You must start off as fast and as hard as you can when the ball is snapped. You do this to set up the defender. You want him to worry about your running right past him and catching a long pass.

The second thing a receiver must do to get open is to make very sharp and very quick cuts. When you cut, plant your push–off foot and cut directly. Don't round off your move and give the defender a chance to recover and stay with you.

practicing on your own

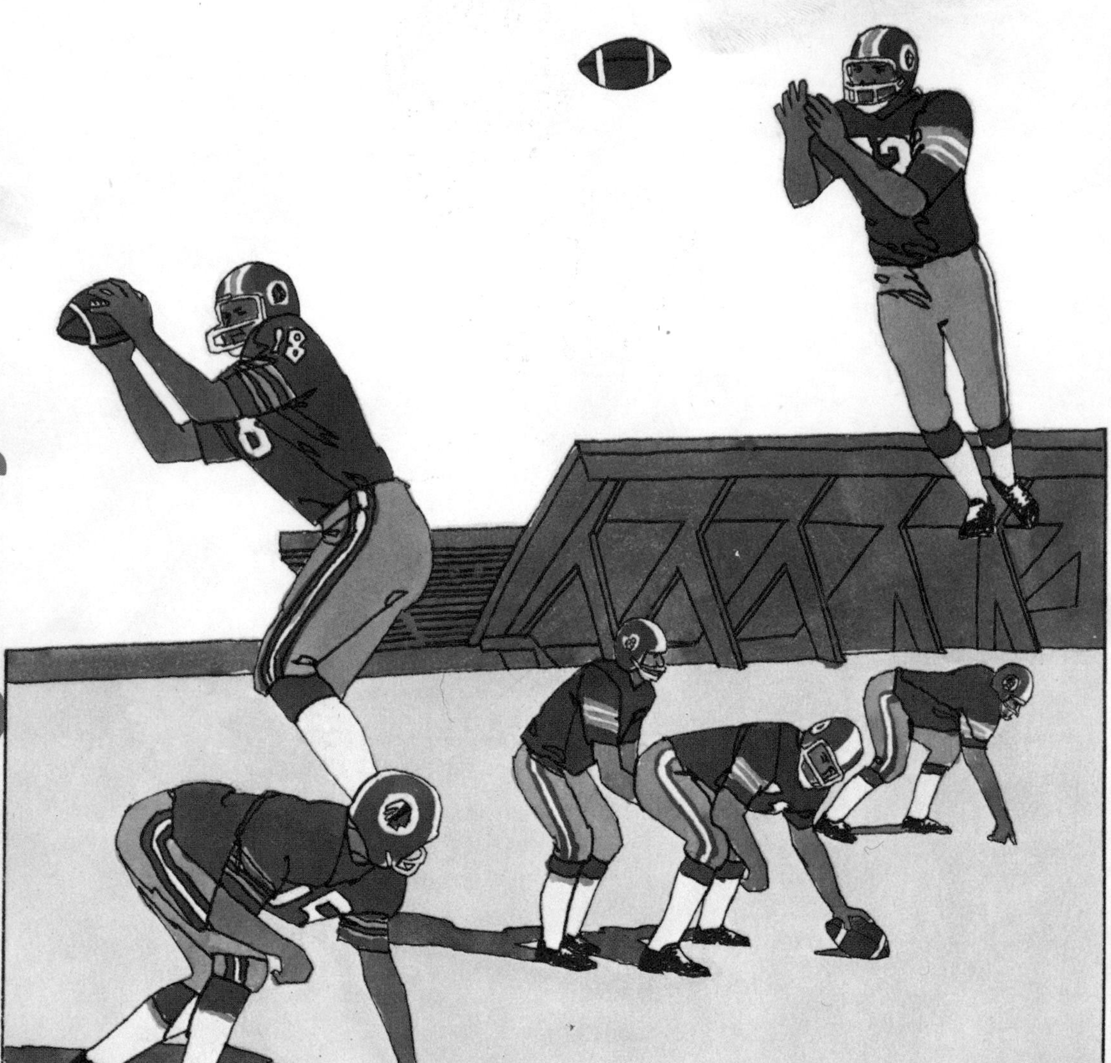

The only way you can improve your physical skills is practice. If you want to catch passes, you need someone to throw to you. Work on your concentration. Learn to look the ball into your hands. Practice tucking the ball away.

Paint a name or number on one of the panels of the football. When you catch the ball, call out the name or number as soon as you can. You really have to see the ball to do this quickly.

It is also important to work at catching balls in all kinds of positions. Ask your passer to throw high, low, and to either side of you. Tell him to make you dive for some catches.

Remember: Catch the Ball with your hands.

creative
education
sports
instructional
series for
young
people